THE HIDDEN STORY OF
ALCOHOLISM

Ella Newell

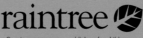

raintree

a Capstone company — publishers for children

Raintree is an imprint of Capstone Global Library Limited, a company incorporated in England and Wales having its registered office at 264 Banbury Road, Oxford OX2 7DY – Registered company number: 6695582

www.raintree.co.uk
myorders@raintree.co.uk

Text © Capstone Global Library Limited 2016
The moral rights of the proprietor have been asserted.

Produced for Raintree by Calcium
Edited by Sarah Eason and Jen Sanderson
Designed by Keith Williams
Picture research by Sarah Eason
Production by Victoria Fitzgerald
Originated by Capstone Global Library Ltd © 2016
Printed and bound in China

ISBN 978 1 4747 1634 5
19 18 17 16 15
10 9 8 7 6 5 4 3 2 1

British Library Cataloguing in Publication Data
A full catalogue record for this book is available from the British Library.

Acknowledgements
We would like to thank the following for permission to reproduce photographs: Dreamstime: Awhelin 42, Monkeybusinessimages 28, Yuri Arcurs 44; Shutterstock: AlenKadr 24, Aaron Amat 7, Baloncici 12, Radu Bercan 15, Bikeriderlondon 19, 29, Diego Cervo 25, Creatista 14, Maria Dryfhout 27, Sebastian Duda 6, Dutourdumonde 10, Fanfo 4, Featureflash 40, 41, Lakov Filimonov 16, Dmitry Kalinovsky 22, Karramba Production 23, Monkey Business Images 34, Pavel L Photo and Video 38, William Perugini 5, Photo Works 36 andreas Saldavs 32, Carlos E. Santa Maria 8, Olaf Speier 20, Gert Very 31.

Cover photographs reproduced with permission of: Shutterstock: Ilike.

Every effort has been made to contact copyright holders of material reproduced in this book. Any omissions will be rectified in subsequent printings if notice is given to the publisher.

Some words are shown in bold, **like this**. You can find out what they mean by looking in the glossary.

CONTENTS

THE TRUTH ABOUT ALCOHOLISM

Glasses of champagne raised in celebration at weddings; cans of beer enjoyed at a barbecue on a hot, sunny day – alcohol is all around us, in pubs and cafés and on sale in shops. Many adults enjoy an **alcoholic** drink from time to time without a problem. For others, alcohol becomes a problem that causes them and their families long-term damage.

This book examines what alcohol is and what it does to a person's body. It looks at the feelings, facts and figures behind why people drink and what can happen when they drink too much. Delving deep behind the news headlines, the book looks at the truth of the problems and dangers of **alcohol abuse**.

It is traditional to enjoy a glass of champagne on special occasions, but many people choose non-alcoholic drinks.

BREAKING NEWS

>> The NHS estimates that around 9 per cent of men in the United Kingdom and 4 per cent of women show signs of alcohol dependence.

KNOWING THE RISKS

Being aware of the warning signs of alcohol abuse can help an individual and his or her family and friends to seek support. They may then get help before the problem becomes serious. People can make full recoveries from alcohol abuse. Recognizing the cause of their problems is vital to helping them stay well and healthy without misusing alcohol in the long term.

It is likely that many young people will find themselves in situations where alcohol is offered or available. It is important to be aware of the risks and dangers of underage drinking in order to be able to deal with such situations.

Many people drink alcohol without problems when they are socializing. However, for some people, alcohol becomes a problem that causes physical and emotional harm.

CHAPTER ONE

ALL ABOUT ALCOHOL

Kate is a mother of two and has always worked as a nurse. Sometimes, she has a drink at the weekend while she is relaxing, perhaps sharing a bottle of wine when friends visit. Kate also occasionally likes a beer when she watches sport on television.

Fifteen-year-old Safraz had never been **drunk** before. One blisteringly hot day, he was hanging out with a group of friends near a river. One of his friends had brought some vodka and soda water. Safraz was not really interested in drinking

Many adults enjoy the different tastes of alcoholic drinks and the way alcohol makes them feel when they drink a small amount.

BREAKING NEWS

>> A survey completed in 2012 showed that more than 9 million people in England drink more than the recommended daily limits. The recommended daily limits are four units for men and three units

alcohol but he did not want to look foolish in front of his friends, by not doing what they were doing. He hated the taste of the alcohol but the **mixers** made it taste better, so he gulped it down. Safraz and a girl decided to jump off a bridge into the river to cool down. The girl surfaced, but Safraz was not a strong swimmer. The effect of the alcohol had slowed and confused his reactions. He never surfaced.

SAFE DRINKING

Many people, like Kate, can safely drink a sensible amount of alcohol without harming themselves. However, the effect of alcohol on some people, like Safraz, is to make them drink and behave in a dangerous way, sometimes with tragic consequences.

Some young people choose not to drink alcohol, preferring juice and soft drinks.

for women. One alcohol unit is measured as 10 ml or 8 g of pure alcohol. This is equivalent to one 25 ml single measure of whisky, one-third of a pint of beer or half a standard (175 ml) glass of wine.

Alcohol is a drug. It changes the way a person's brain and body works, which affects his or her thoughts and actions.

The scientific name for alcohol is **ethanol**. It can be made in different ways, but the most common method used to make alcohol is a process called **fermentation**. During the process, a fungus called yeast breaks down sugar and turns it into alcohol.

USES OF ALCOHOL
Some forms of alcohol are also used in cleaning products, such as soap and deodorant. Alcohol is used as an antiseptic and can even be used as a fuel to power cars.

The body's reaction to alcohol depends on a person's age, weight, sex, fitness, the amount of food consumed and any medication he or she has taken.

Alcohol can be very dangerous. It can be fatal to drink alcohol that is not meant for consumption.

DIFFERENT DRINKS

Beer is made from barley, hops, water and sugar. Wine comes from sugary grapes. Spirits such as whisky are made using fermentation and an additional process called **distillation**. In distillation, ethanol is reduced to a stronger liquid, which increases the strength of the alcohol. Ingredients and colours are added to make different alcoholic drinks.

The strength of an alcoholic drink depends on how much pure alcohol or ethanol it contains. On bottled and canned alcoholic drink labels, this is usually shown as the percentage of alcohol by volume or ABV.

UNDERCOVER STORY

SIZE MATTERS

When a person takes a **breathalyzer** test, the amount of alcohol in his or her body is measured. This is known as Blood Alcohol Concentration (BAC) and is usually measured by dividing the grams of alcohol by 100 millilitres of blood. If a middle-aged, large man and a young, small woman drink the same amount of alcohol, the effect on them will be very different and their BAC will be different, too. The effect of alcohol on the body depends on age, sex, size and the amount of food a person has eaten. In England, Wales and Northern Ireland, the law considers a person to be over an acceptable level of alcohol if his or her BAC is 80 milligrams of alcohol to 100 millilitres of blood. In Scotland, the limit is 50 milligrams.

When someone drinks an alcoholic drink, around 20 per cent of it passes straight through the stomach and into the bloodstream. Once there, it can reach the brain within minutes. A full stomach slows down the speed at which alcohol is absorbed, which is why it is safer to drink after eating. Around 80 per cent of alcohol passes into the small intestine. From there it travels around the body, affecting major organs, including the brain, liver, heart and kidneys.

Tributes were left to singer Amy Winehouse after her death from accidental alcohol poisoning.

BODY AND MIND

Alcohol spreads to the central nervous system, which is responsible for **coordination**. This is why a person often finds it difficult to balance or walk in a straight line after drinking alcohol. The person's thoughts become muddled and his or her speech may become slurred.

After drinking alcohol, a person's blood vessels expand. This makes eyes look bloodshot and the person's face appear red or flushed. Messages from the brain to the eyes become confused, resulting in blurred vision and an inability to correctly judge speed and distance. Large amounts of alcohol can also irritate the stomach, causing stomach pains, vomiting and diarrhoea.

The frontal part of a person's brain is in charge of emotions. As alcohol affects this part of the brain, a person may become more emotional and may cry or be overly friendly towards strangers. Alcohol reduces **inhibitions,** making people do things they would not usually do.

HITTING THE HEADLINES

AMY WINEHOUSE

Talented 27-year-old singer Amy Winehouse had a history of drug and alcohol problems. She had sought help for her issues and had not drunk alcohol for several months. However, a few days before her death, Amy began drinking once more. She died alone, having drunk too much. Alcohol can poison a person if he or she drinks too much. Signs of alcohol poisoning include confusion, vomiting, irregular breathing, seizures and pale or blue skin. The individual may also seem to be conscious but does not respond when spoken to or shaken. A person with alcohol poisoning may also become unconscious. Without immediate medical treatment, a person can die from alcohol poisoning.

People often drink alcohol to enjoy its relaxing effect. However, too much alcohol can make people moody and irritable. People often suffer from hangovers the day after consuming a lot of alcohol. A hangover is the body's reaction to the toxic, or poisonous, effects of alcohol. Symptoms include a headache, dry mouth, bad breath, aches, tiredness and nausea.

Alcohol abuse is when an individual's drinking begins to cause harm to himself or herself and negatively affects family and friends. Relationships may break down, work suffers and the person's behaviour may become aggressive, risky or irresponsible. A person may also develop serious alcohol-related health problems.

It can take several hours for alcohol to leave the body and much longer to recover from the effects of drinking too much.

ALCOHOL PROBLEMS

When a person is **addicted** to or dependent on alcohol, he or she is suffering from **alcoholism**. Alcoholism is when a person feels unable to cope without a regular drink or needs a drink before carrying out everyday tasks, such as household chores or a job.

Any alcohol problem can have a devastating effect on the individual, family and friends. Being aware of the warning signs of alcoholism or other alcohol abuse can help sufferers and friends recognize the problem before it becomes too severe and may help them to get the support they need.

UNDERCOVER STORY

HEAVY DRINKING

Binge drinking is drinking a large amount of alcohol in a short period of time. Some people think binge drinking is harmless. They believe that because they drink heavily only occasionally, they are not in danger of becoming addicted to alcohol. However, binge drinking can be very dangerous.

The liver metabolizes, or breaks down, most of the alcohol a person drinks, but an average adult can break down only about 8 grams of alcohol per hour. If the body cannot cope with the alcohol in its system and the liver cannot break it down, a person becomes unwell. In the worst cases, someone may choke to death on his or her vomit or fall into an alcoholic coma.

CHAPTER TWO

TEENAGE DRINKING

Kayleigh was doing well at school and had a good group of friends. Then she started dating a new boyfriend who was a few years older than her. Kayleigh began drinking, using a fake ID to get into clubs and bars. She drank to keep up with the other friends in her boyfriend's group. Soon, Kayleigh was waking up most mornings with terrible hangovers. She stopped seeing her good friends and became isolated from her family. Kayleigh was unhappy and her new relationship broke down. Instead of turning to her old friends and family for support, Kayleigh drowned her sorrows in alcohol. She dropped out of school. One evening, a family friend found her crying in the street. Her bag had been stolen and no cab driver would give her a lift. Instead of a healthy-looking, happy girl, Kayleigh looked like a mess. Fortunately for Kayleigh, her family got her the help she needed and she was able to return to school.

Drinking too much alcohol can fuel aggressive behaviour.

BREAKING NEWS

>> Although the legal drinking age in the United Kingdom is 18 years, in 2003, 61 per cent of school pupils aged 11 to 15 years, had drunk alcohol at

Although there are laws preventing the sale of alcohol to those under 18 in the United Kingdom, many young people drink regularly.

UNDERAGE DRINKING

According to Institute of Alcohol Studies (IAS), the United Kingdom ranks highly among the worst offenders in Europe for underage drinking. The IAS says that in the long run, the age at which a person starts drinking alcohol plays a significant part in determining the chances of him or her developing alcohol-related problems later in life. A study in the United States showed that those who started drinking before the age of 15 were four times more likely to develop an alcohol dependency than those who began drinking at the age of 21.

least once. However, in 2012, according to statistics from the Health & Social Care Information Centre (HSCIC), this figure had dropped to 43 per cent.

Why do young people want to drink alcohol? Adolescents go through many physical and emotional changes as they mature into adults. Part of this process is discovering their identity and developing independence. Experimenting and looking for new experiences is a natural part of growing up. Many teenagers are eager to try alcohol, but it is important that they are aware of the risks of underage drinking. It is also necessary to understand the reasons why young people are not allowed to drink until they are a certain age.

Teenage years are exciting, challenging and sometimes difficult. Some young people may drink alcohol to avoid facing family or other problems, but this only makes the situation worse.

DANGEROUS INFLUENCES

Young people may see adults relaxing and enjoying a drink in a pub or at home, and think drinking alcohol is harmless fun. Many teenagers think that if people around them drink, then why should they not do it, too? Films and advertisements often show people drinking, seemingly without problems.

It is often easy for young people to get alcohol, even though it is illegal. In 2014, the HSCIC said that under half (44 per cent) of all school pupils who drank alcohol said they bought it. Those who had bought alcohol had usually done so from friends, someone other than family or friends, off-licences or shops or supermarkets.

If a teenager spends time with friends who are older, he or she may feel pressure to behave and act in a similar way. Other teens may tease a person if she or he does not fit in. This **peer** pressure can be hard to resist.

Sometimes, people start drinking to escape from unhappiness in their lives. However, drinking alcohol only leads to more difficulties and problems.

UNDERCOVER STORY
HARD LEMONADE

Sweet drinks, such as lemonade or fruit juice, can be mixed with alcohol. These sweet drinks are targeted at young teenagers, who prefer the sweet taste of soft drinks to the more bitter taste of other alcoholic drinks, such as beer. These drinks can be dangerously deceptive – they may taste sweet and harmless, but they are loaded with alcohol.

Alcohol can permanently and irreversibly damage a young person's brain. Until the age of 20, a person's brain is not fully developed. At this crucial stage, alcohol can interfere with the brain's "wiring", leading to thought and memory problems in adulthood. It can also make a young person more likely to become addicted to alcohol when he or she is older. The World Health Organization (WHO) suggests that drinking alcohol before 14 years of age carries an increased risk for alcohol dependence and abuse at later ages.

These are just some of the many reasons why underage drinking is especially dangerous and is illegal in most countries. The risks involved are higher than those for adults. The teenage body and mind is still in a crucial phase of development, so the long-term consequences of underage drinking are more severe.

HITTING THE HEADLINES

ENERGY ALERT

A recent report suggests that mixing energy drinks with alcohol can be even more dangerous than drinking alcohol on its own. Energy drinks are popular with many teenagers because the caffeine in them gives the drinker a "buzz". Drinking just one energy drink with alcohol may have the same result as drinking one bottle of wine and several cups of coffee. The caffeine in the energy drink is thought to make a person less aware of how drunk he or she is.

BREAKING NEWS

>> In the United Kingdom from 2012 to 2013, there were 1,008,850 hospital admissions related to the drinking of alcohol.

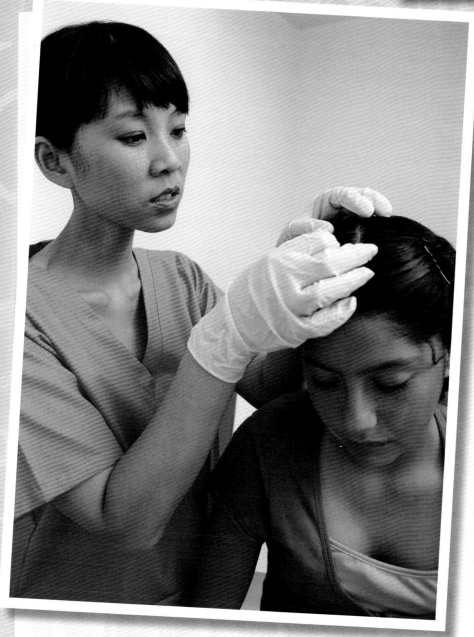

Accident and emergency rooms have to deal with injuries from alcohol-related accidents or fights. Tragically, some of these incidents may be fatal.

In 2012, there were 8,367 deaths in the United Kingdom directly related to alcohol consumption.

Drinking can have a negative effect on teenagers' schoolwork, social life and friendships, as well as their general health. Heavy or regular drinking affects every area of a person's life – there may be many changes in the person's behaviour, mood, appearance and health, even when he or she is not drunk.

Underage drinking is illegal. Off-licences and supermarkets can be prosecuted for selling alcohol to underage drinkers. As a result, teenagers often obtain alcohol from people who have no care or interest in their well-being. A teenager may start to mix with a new crowd, begin to play truant

A young person may begin to mix with a new "drinking" crowd and withdraw from close and trusted friends.

and avoid good friends who choose not to drink alcohol. Some young people may steal from parents or guardians to pay for alcohol.

CHANGING BEHAVIOUR
Young people who are drinking heavily often withdraw from family and friends and spend more time alone. They will often lose interest in sports and hobbies. Young people with an alcohol problem may put on a lot of weight and care little about their appearance.

The energy levels of heavy drinkers will be lower, so schoolwork may suffer. Concentration and memory are affected and people often feel physically unwell, too.

Regular drinking builds up a person's **tolerance** to alcohol. This means an individual needs to drink more alcohol for the same effect. However, drinking more increases the harm done to the body and the likelihood of developing a serious problem related to alcohol.

HITTING THE HEADLINES
DANIEL RADCLIFFE

Harry Potter star Daniel Radcliffe stopped drinking alcohol at the age of 20 when he realized that he was becoming dependent on drinking and it was spiralling out of control. Speaking on the BBC television programme *Newsbeat*, the young actor acknowledged that drinking was not bringing him happiness. He said, "I drank in search of happiness … I've drunk a lot but I'm still not happy … There is a lot of pressure on young people … to find happiness through going out and getting mashed."

Parents often complain that their teenagers are impulsive and have no sense of danger. Well, this is partly due to a biological cause! Scientists believe teenagers' brains are not yet fully mature, including the parts of the brain that are responsible for awareness of risk. Drinking alcohol muddles judgement and decision-making ability, which makes teenagers even more likely to underestimate danger and make poor choices.

Drinking and driving is incredibly dangerous. No matter how capable the driver feels, he or she will not be able to react quickly.

Sometimes, young people will drink in secret places, such as near rivers or lakes, hidden from view because they know they are not supposed to be drinking. However, this is dangerous because there is no one to help if a problem occurs. Many young victims of drowning accidents had been drinking.

Opposite: People often say they are able to drive when they have been drinking. This is not the case. Alcohol slows down reactions and awareness and makes it unsafe to drive.

BREAKING NEWS

>> According to the Department for Transport, in 2012, drink-drive accidents accounted for 16 per cent of all road deaths in Britain.

SAFE DRIVING

Driving safely depends on instant, clear judgements, clear vision and thinking, and rapid reactions. Drinking alcohol affects all of these skills. Drinking and driving is a recipe for disaster. The driver may lose his or her licence and possibly end up in prison. Even worse, he or she may cause an accident in which passengers, passers-by, other drivers or him- or herself are seriously injured or killed. A person should never get in a car driven by someone who appears to have been drinking.

HITTING THE HEADLINES
DRUNK DRIVING

Olympian Michael Phelps was arrested and charged in September 2013 with driving under the influence of alcohol. A judge placed him on probation and if caught again, Phelps will go to prison.

Studies have shown that young people who start drinking before the age of 15 are 11 times more likely to be in a physical fight after drinking. Some people react aggressively and violently when drunk. They may regret their actions the following day or may not even remember how they behaved.

and alcohol. This may be because people become more aggressive when drunk. People who are drunk are less able to deal effectively with difficult situations that could put them in danger. Their slower and more confused reactions mean they may become involved in dangerous or risky situations.

Many people believe that there is a link between alcohol abuse and domestic abuse, when one partner is violent and cruel towards the other partner or another family member. However, being drunk is no excuse for hurting a loved one.

There is often a link between crime

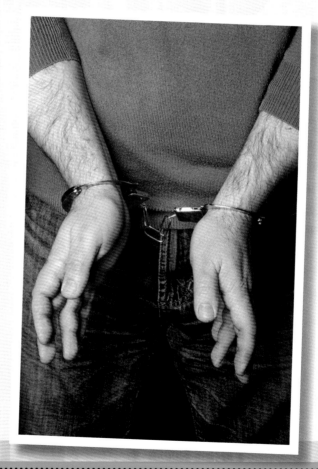

A moment of drunken anger or stupidity can lead to prosecution.

BREAKING NEWS

>> One-fifth of all violent incidents in 2010 to 2011 took place in or around a pub or nightclub. More than two-thirds of violent offences occur in the evening or at night and 45 per cent at the weekend.

DANGEROUS SITUATIONS

Drinking too much alcohol also makes people more vulnerable and regrettably, others may take advantage of their situation. People who drink heavily are more likely than non-drinkers to become the victims of crime. This is perhaps because they find themselves in situations that get out of hand and cannot be easily controlled.

If someone does not recognize the warning signs of a possible problem or is unable to react swiftly, he or she will be an easier target for a criminal attack. This includes rape or other assaults.

Being drunk can also lead to casual and unsafe sex that a person may regret the next day.

Being drunk means being less aware of danger and risk.

CHAPTER THREE

PROBLEMS WITH ALCOHOL

In 1995, golfer John Daly won one of golf's most prestigious tournaments: the British Open. To many, Daly had it all – success, fame and money. Or did he? In March 2008, Daly's coach quit. About Daly he reportedly said, "The most important thing in his life is getting drunk." In October 2008, Daly was taken into custody after being found drunk outside a restaurant. The police released his mugshot (photograph of his face) to the media, which resulted in negative publicity. Daly stopped drinking alcohol and has seen his golf improve. He has said that much of his past struggle with alcohol was a result of growing up with an alcoholic father.

UNDERCOVER STORY

IT CAN HAPPEN TO ANYONE

The traditional stereotype of an alcoholic is a person who lives on the streets, with no money or family. While there are many people like that, there are also many people who manage to hold down good jobs while covering up their alcoholism. Although they may seem fine on the outside, their health suffers and so do their relationships.

ALCOHOL PROBLEMS

Many adults are able to enjoy alcohol in moderation without any problems. However, when someone's drinking is out of control, like John Daly's, he or she is caught in a cycle of alcohol abuse. Alcohol abuse can affect anyone and there is no single reason for it. Someone may start drinking more alcohol after a traumatic event or the loss of a loved one. He or she may use alcohol to feel more confident. Sometimes, a dependency on alcohol can develop into alcoholism when someone becomes physically and emotionally unable to manage without an alcoholic drink.

Anyone who regularly drinks too much is at risk of becoming an alcoholic.

In 2005, Tom Ward, a 19-year-old University of Hull student, took part in an **initiation ceremony** for rugby team recruits. The ceremony included a pub crawl in which every 10 minutes, teams of students set off for a pub. The teams had five minutes to down pints and spirits before running to the next pub. The aim was to stay ahead of the next team.

Ward, a second-year student, consumed at least 12 pints and up to six shots in three hours. After arriving back at his student house, he fell and was discovered lifeless at the foot of the stairs. Attempts to revive him failed. A coroner at Hull ruled that Ward had suffocated as a result of being drunk.

The body cannot cope with too much alcohol in a short time.

Opposite: Going to university is an exciting time, but some young people can feel pressured into drinking too much, sometimes with terrible consequences.

In 2012, 19-year-old American student David Bogenberger died of alcohol poisoning after enduring a two-hour initiation rite in which he was made to drink large amounts of alcohol in a short time. The friend he was with managed to survive the ordeal.

HITTING THE HEADLINES

INITIATION RITES

The terrible deaths of Tom Ward and David Bogenberger were part of initiation rites known as "**hazing**". Hazing takes place around the world and is potentially illegal, cruel and very dangerous. It puts a person under emotional and physical stress and is a type of bullying. An alarming number of initiation rites include alcohol hazing. This rite is incredibly dangerous and deeply cruel.

BINGE DRINKING

Some people think that if they drink large amounts of alcohol, but only rarely, then they are safe from the dangers of alcohol. They believe the only side effect of heavy drinking will be a bad hangover. They are wrong. Drinking a lot in a short time puts stress on the body and it can be fatal.

The World Health Organization states, "Alcohol is the world's third-largest risk factor for disease burden [impact of a health problem in terms of financial cost and deaths]. Four per cent of all deaths worldwide are attributable to alcohol. The harmful use of alcohol is especially fatal for younger age groups and alcohol is the world's leading risk factor for death among males aged 15–59." Some alcohol-related problems, such as weight gain, can be reversed, but others, such as liver disease, cannot. The liver is the organ that breaks down most of the alcohol a person drinks. This makes the organ vulnerable to harm through alcohol misuse. Long-term drinking kills off liver cells, leading to a disease called cirrhosis. Long-term excessive drinking can also lead to liver cancer, heart disease and high blood pressure. Alcohol interferes with the delicate workings of the brain and can cause short- and long-term memory problems.

UNDERCOVER STORY

MENTAL WELL-BEING

Anxiety, depression and other mental health issues can develop when people become dependent on alcohol, because alcohol causes chemical changes to the brain. People sometimes continue drinking or drink even more to overcome these feelings, but this only makes the problems worse. Any relief is only temporary and the vicious cycle of drink and depression continues.

BREAKING NEWS

>> Although alcohol does not contain any fat, it is very fattening! It has no nutritional value but contains a lot of calories. If you do not burn up these calories, they turn to fat. One pint of lager has more calories than a Fun Size Snickers® bar!

ALCOHOL AND PREGNANCY

Foetal alcohol syndrome can affect newborns whose mothers drink too much alcohol during pregnancy. It can result in babies having abnormal facial features and behavioural problems. Some studies suggest that a woman can drink a small amount of alcohol while pregnant, while others recommend no alcohol at all during pregnancy.

The effects of alcohol on a baby can be devastating, causing lifelong problems such as poor memory and learning difficulties.

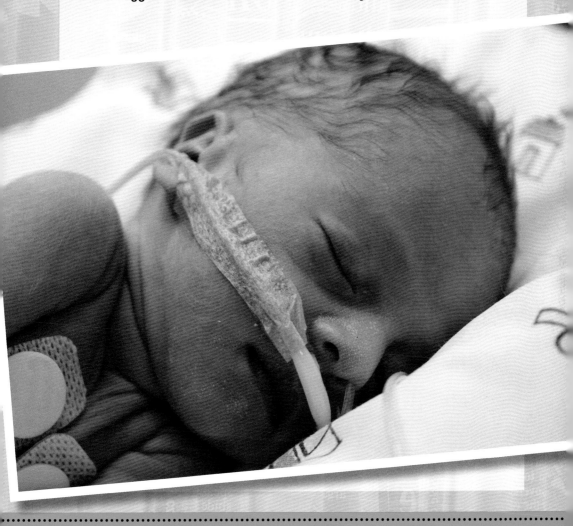

Alcohol abuse hurts everyone involved, not just the individual sufferer. Families often crack under the pressure of one parent drinking. His or her behaviour may be unpredictable and even violent. A parent may be unable to care properly for a child. In some instances, a child may be taken away from the parent or guardian with an alcohol problem for his or her protection.

A drinking problem affects a person's performance at work.

BREAKING NEWS

>> In 2013, more than 2.5 million children in the United Kingdom, including 90,000 babies, were living with a parent who drank alcohol to hazardous levels.

ALCOHOL AND WORK

Going to work with a hangover, secretly drinking at work, being unable to focus on the task at hand – these are just some of the problems that an alcoholic faces in the workplace. Before long, he or she may be unable to hold down a job. Losing a job can lead to losing one's home.

Even if a person is able to continue working, the effects of alcohol abuse can have a terrible impact on close family and friends. Family members may experience many emotions, from fear to anger at a loved one's unpredictable and moody behaviour caused by alcohol abuse.

A child with an alcoholic parent may feel a mix of confusing emotions. He or she may feel guilty, embarrassed and even frightened. It is important for a child in this situation to tell a trusted adult, who can help the parent and the child find the support they need. It is important, too, to remember that the child is in no way to blame for the parent's problem.

HITTING THE HEADLINES

A FAMILY PROBLEM

A child whose parent is an alcoholic is more likely to develop an alcohol problem than children of parents who are not alcoholics. This is partly due to **genetic** links and partly to the family environment in which the child is brought up. However, a lot of young people who live with an alcoholic parent do not develop alcohol problems. Being aware of the risks and finding support to cope with difficulties can help prevent any later alcohol abuse.

CHAPTER FOUR

GETTING HELP

Anne had been drinking heavily for months. It started when her marriage broke up. Her eldest daughter, Nicola, took on much of the care for herself and her younger brother when Anne was too hungover or too unhappy to get them ready for school. Although Anne loved her children very much, life at home was chaotic. None of Nicola's friends were allowed by their parents to come and stay over for her birthday party. One of the parents even told Anne that they did not feel safe leaving their children in her care. It was at this time that Anne finally admitted she had to address her problem.

Often it takes a specific incident for an alcoholic to realize that he or she needs help.

FIRST STEPS

The first step to recovery for an alcoholic is admitting to having a problem. This can often be the hardest step. The individual may feel fear or shame about his or her bad behaviour when drunk and may not even want to face up to the truth. Once a person admits and recognizes the problem, he or she can start to get the support needed to recover.

If a young person lives with someone who has an alcohol problem, there are people who can offer support to him or her. It is important for a young person to talk to a trusted adult about the problems at home.

UNDERCOVER STORY

WARNING SIGNS

There are several warning signs that someone is developing a problem with alcohol. These include:

- Relying on alcohol to have fun, forget problems or relax
- Withdrawing from friends or family
- Drinking alone
- Losing interest in hobbies and activities
- Needing to drink more to get the same effect as the body builds up a tolerance to alcohol
- Lying or stealing to get money for alcohol
- Wanting to stop drinking but feeling unable to do so
- Binge drinking.

People who have an alcohol problem need help to change their behaviour around alcohol. This may be treatment in rehab, counselling or support programmes. A young person who thinks he or she has an alcohol problem or feels in danger of developing one, needs to know that there is help available at any stage. Even if a young drinker knows he or she has broken the law by drinking alcohol, there are plenty of ways to change the situation and there is a lot of support available. There is also help for those who engage in negative behaviour linked to alcohol abuse.

A judge ordered actress Lindsay Lohan to wear an alcohol-detection bracelet and attend alcohol education classes after drunk driving incidents. The actress no longer drinks.

SUPPORTING RECOVERY

There are many different treatments and approaches to dealing with an alcohol problem. Each depends upon the individual and the type and severity of his or her alcohol problem. Some people need to spend time in rehab, others may follow a programme to support alcoholics, and others will see a counsellor. Many alcoholics need to stay **sober** (not drink alcohol at all) for the rest of their lives.

People may often suffer from unpleasant **withdrawal** symptoms when giving up alcohol, because the body and mind crave what they have become used to. People who give up drinking alcohol also need to develop positive ways to cope with their feelings and the personal issues that may have initially made them turn to alcohol. With help, people can make full and long-lasting recoveries from alcohol abuse.

HITTING THE HEADLINES

ALCOHOL BRACELET

Some people who have often been in trouble with the law as a result of their drunken behaviour are issued special bracelets to make sure they do not drink alcohol. This is an alternative to being sent to prison. The bracelet is attached to the person's ankle and it soaks up the individual's sweat. Readings from the bracelet are taken every 30 minutes and the data is then transmitted to a database. Trained staff monitor and interpret the data, looking for signs of alcohol consumption and tampering with the device.

CHAPTER FIVE

SOCIETY AND ALCOHOL

The scene: a beautiful woman sits at a bar, drinking. A handsome man joins her and they laugh and smile, enjoying their drinks. The bartender fills their glasses. Everyone in the bar is drinking and seems happy and healthy.

The average person in Britain spends almost £50,000 on alcohol during their lifetime, which is around £787 a year.

MADE TO LOOK COOL

This scene has been played out in thousands of films and television programmes and advertisements. Alcohol is often shown as an acceptable and attractive way to add to a social occasion or relax after a hard day at work. Many people believe that this presentation is a negative influence on young people. They say that it encourages young people to associate alcohol with being cool and having a good time.

Society's attitude to alcohol is often confusing. Alcohol is a drug, but it is sold and advertised widely and many adults drink alcohol. Understanding the risks and dangers of alcohol to the young body and mind can help teenagers to make sense of why alcohol is illegal until a certain age. Knowledge can also help them to make safe and sensible choices.

UNDERCOVER STORY

GLAMORIZING DRINKING

According to a research review in the journal *Alcohol and Alcoholism*, alcohol advertising and marketing increases the likelihood that young people will start drinking, or that they will drink more if they are already consuming alcohol. Russia has banned the advertising of alcohol in all media in an attempt to deal with the country's alcohol problem. According to the WHO, one in five men in the Russian Federation and neighbouring countries dies from an alcohol-related problem.

Although many people around the world drink alcohol, a higher percentage of people currently do not drink at all. According to the World Health Organization, 48 per cent of the world's adult population have not drunk alcohol. It is important to remember that people do not need to drink in order to have a good time.

Many people choose not to drink alcohol at all or decide to stop drinking it for various reasons. Some people do not drink because they do not like the taste of alcohol. Others do not drink because they do not like being unable to control their behaviour.

Many celebrities, such as Jada Pinkett Smith, choose not to drink alcohol.

UNDERCOVER STORY

YOU DON'T HAVE TO DRINK

Support other friends who do not want to drink. Be bold and proud about asking for soft drinks. True friends will not put someone under pressure to drink. Focus on other activities that make you feel good. Do not feel embarrassed about your stance. Be clear about your choices. Never get into a car with someone who has been drinking. Be critical of the "cool" image of alcohol in advertising and films – and think about the real effects of alcohol.

ALCOHOL-FREE

Kelly Osbourne was thrust into the limelight when she was still a teenager. She gave up alcohol in 2009 after three stints in rehab. At the age of 18, singer-songwriter Jessie J suffered a minor stroke. As a result, she does not drink.

Some young people tell their friends that they drink alcohol to impress others. The reality is that most young people choose not to drink alcohol. In 2011, the NHS reported that 55 per cent of 11 to 16-year-olds had said they had never had an alcoholic drink.

Some people, such as Fearne Cotton, avoid alcohol because of its effect on physical appearance and general health.

In 1920, in an attempt to end alcohol-related crime, the United States became a "dry" country – prohibiting the sale of alcohol or "intoxicating liquor". National Prohibition was meant to remove the crime associated with the many bars, saloons and clubs that had grown up in towns and cities across the United States. However, Prohibition drove alcohol underground. Making and selling alcohol became a criminal and profitable industry. The law was eventually changed as a result, but some communities in the United States still remain dry to this day.

Parts of the state of Virginia in the United States are "dry", meaning that people are not allowed to buy or sell alcohol there.

RELIGION AND ALCOHOL

Some countries do not allow alcohol as part of their religious and cultural beliefs. Alcoholic drinks are banned in the Islamic religion, although in some Islamic countries it is possible to buy and drink alcohol. In others, such as Saudi Arabia, drinking alcohol is forbidden and can result in a long prison sentence or a public lashing.

Cheap alcohol has created problems in many countries, including the United Kingdom and Australia. Young people flood into town centres at weekends and buy cheap alcohol with the main intention of becoming as drunk as possible. This leads to crime waves, accidents and serious social problems. Politicians are discussing ways to make alcohol harder to access in order to lessen the problems.

UNDERCOVER STORY

VISITS TO A&E

Although underage drinking is illegal, according to research, nearly 300 children aged 11 and under were admitted to A&E in 2012–13. This figure rose to 6,500 for those under the age of 18. In the past, more boys were admitted but recent figures show that this has changed and now more girls are being admitted. Most drunk teenagers too cannot give the ambulance crew their exact location, making the paramedics' job harder. Many have vomited, with the vomit going into their lungs. Hypothermia is also common. Many girls also claim that they "may have" been sexually assaulted but were too drunk to be sure.

ALCOHOL - THE WHOLE STORY

Many people enjoy drinking alcohol, but as with any drug, use of alcohol can easily develop into a serious problem. That is why it is important to be aware of the risks and to be alert to signs of alcohol abuse. Around the world, there is much debate about the use and misuse of alcohol. Different cultures and countries often have very different views towards alcohol. Some people believe alcohol is just as harmful as illegal drugs. They think that alcoholic drinks should not be easily available to young people.

People can have fun without drinking alcohol.

MAKING CHOICES

In countries and cultures where alcohol is an accepted part of everyday life, there is concern about the cost of dealing with health and social problems caused by alcohol misuse. In these countries, the authorities are now using different ways to raise alcohol awareness and encourage only sensible drinking. The social cost of alcohol misuse is huge, with alcohol-related crime and health problems costing countries vast amounts of money. As we learn more about the teenage brain, we are discovering more about the specific and long-term risks of underage drinking.

The more people are aware of the dangers and risks of alcohol abuse, the better equipped they are to make safe and sensible decisions about their drinking. The more people find other activities in their lives to make them feel good, the less they may need to rely on alcohol.

The truth is that many young people enjoy their lives to the fullest without ever needing to drink alcohol.

UNDERCOVER STORY

ANYONE, ANYWHERE

Alcohol problems can affect anyone, whatever his or her ethnicity, sex or status. There is no quick fix for alcohol abuse. The difficulties of recovery are the same for a celebrity or a nurse.

GLOSSARY

addicted when the body and mind of an individual crave and depend on particular substances

alcohol abuse harmful or out of control drinking

alcoholic person addicted to alcohol

alcoholism condition in which a person has become addicted to alcohol

binge drinking drinking a large amount of alcohol in a short period of time

breathalyzer breath test to see if a driver is over the limit for the legal amount of alcohol in the body for driving

calorie units of energy in food

coordination different parts of the body working together effectively

distillation process by which ethanol is made stronger

drunk consumed too much alcohol

ethanol scientific name for alcohol

fermentation process by which yeast and sugar turns into alcohol

genetic having to do with genes, the building blocks of an individual's body

hazing initiation rite that sometimes involves drinking large amounts of alcohol in a short space of time

inhibition feeling that makes one stop doing something

initiation ceremony something people are asked to do before being allowed to join certain groups or clubs

mixer drink added, or mixed, with alcohol

peer someone of a similar age

sober not drunk

tolerance ability to cope with something

withdrawal stopping

FIND OUT MORE

BOOKS

A Little Book of Alcohol: Activities to Explore Alcohol Issues with Young People, Vanessa Rogers (Jessica Kingsley Publishers, 2012)

Binge Drinking (Straight Talk About...), James Bow (Crabtree Publishing, 2015)

I Have an Alcoholic Parent. Now What? (Teen Life 411), Terry Teague Meyer (Rosen Young Adult, 2015)

Keeping Safe Around Alcohol, Drugs and Cigarettes, Anne Rooney (Franklin Watts, 2014)

ORGANIZATIONS

Al-Anon
Helpline: 020 7403 0888
Al-Anon offers support for anyone whose life is, or has been, affected by someone else's drinking problem. Also includes Alateen for teenage friends and relatives of alcoholics.

Drinkaware
Finsbury Circus (Salisbury House)
3rd Floor (Room 519)
London
EC2M 5QQ
Tel: 020 7766 9900
Fax: 020 7504 8217
Website: **www.drinkaware.co.uk**
Drinkaware is a charity that works to reduce alcohol misuse and harm in the United Kingdom.

Adfam
Adfam can help families dealing with alcohol abuse.
Website: **www.adfam.org.uk**

NHS
The NHS Live Well pages have a lot of information on alcohol support.
Website: **www.nhs.uk/Livewell/ alcohol/Pages/Alcoholsupport.aspx**

INDEX